LET'S INVESTIGATE

FOSSIL HUNTING

ph

Published in this edition by Peter Haddock Ltd, Pinfold Lane,
Bridlington, East Yorkshire YO16 5BT

© 1997 Peter Haddock Ltd/Geddes & Grosset Ltd

ISBN 0 7105 0967 7

Printed and bound in India

PART ONE

INTRODUCTION

The study of fossils, which forms a branch of geology or earth science, is called palaeontology. Someone who studies, collects and works with fossils is therefore a palaeontologist, and this can be on a professional or amateur basis. Much of the early study of fossils was undertaken by the French zoologist Georges Cuvier (1769–1832), who recorded the various fossils in the Paris Basin. He realised that the fossils that he found were a record of organisms that had lived a long time ago and that somehow they had been preserved. While his overall interpretation of the evidence uncovered was by no means totally correct he did note that certain fossils or groups of fossils were found at particular levels in the rocks. He was unable to account for the evolution of species and proposed that a series of catastrophes had caused the ending of some organisms. This theory was quickly replaced by proposals from other geologists, such as James Hutton (1726–97), a Scot, and Charles Lyell (1797–1875). This led to a theory called uniformitarianism, which, based on the observed slow rate of geological processes, proposed that the various processes balance each other out over time. Lyell thought that the processes by which mountains were built would eventually be balanced out by their erosion.

These early theories influenced many people, one of whom was Charles Darwin (1809–82), the great English naturalist. By developing and using existing theories and through his pioneering work along the coast of South America, particularly on the Galapagos Islands, Darwin contributed greatly to the idea that life evolved and over an enormous period of time.

The contribution of fossils to the study of evolution has been immense. By careful study and classification, and through the dating of rocks in which fossils are found, it has been possible to help other scientists construct an interlinking tree of organisms from the beginning of life to the present day. In many instances, fossils have provided the missing link in an evolutionary chain of events, but although we are dealing with the direct or indirect remains of organisms that existed millions of years ago, palaeontology is an interesting subject and exciting discoveries are made all the time, some of which question earlier theories.

PART TWO

WHAT IS A FOSSIL?

The word 'fossil' comes from the Latin *fossilis*, which means 'dug up'. A fossil is usually one step or more removed from the original organism, although in certain cases it is the original organism or part of it that is preserved. In all cases, preservation in some form will depend on the remains being buried, usually by mud, silt, fine sand or a similar sediment. In the sea or any other environment that is watery, an organism is likely to be buried quite quickly. When death occurs through age, disease or injury following an attack by a predator, the body sinks to the floor of the sea, lake or pond. If inflowing streams and rivers are carrying large quantities of sediment, then the organism may well be buried. If an organism, animal or plant dies on land, there is less chance of it being covered quickly. It is much more likely to rot or be scavenged, so only in very special circumstances will land organisms be preserved. Fortunately for palaeontologists, such circumstances have occurred in the past, but the bulk of the fossil record is made up of marine organisms, particularly shells similar to those that are so common on our shores today.

When burial has taken place, the sediment thickness

builds up, and eventually this will begin to press down on the developing fossil. At the same time, the soft tissues of the organism will begin to rot and break down and usually decay quite quickly. However, the harder parts, such as the outer shell, or perhaps teeth and bones, withstand these processes and often form the basis of the fossil that is found much later by the fossil hunter. This process of pressing down eventually forms a rock out of the soft sediment. The sediment is said to become *consolidated*, during which all the grains are pushed together (or compacted), and from a mainly sandy sediment a sandstone is formed. Shale and mudstone are formed from silt and mud, and limestone may be made up of shell debris (broken pieces of shell), lime-rich muds and sands. These are all called *sedimentary* rocks because they are made from sediments.

The hard parts that become fossils can be preserved in several ways. The simplest is for the shell or bone to be preserved essentially in its original state. More commonly, some changes will occur. It is frequently the case that waters carrying chemicals in solution percolate or filter through a rock as it is forming. Often, minerals are deposited out of this solution to form the matrix or cement of a rock, which is the binding material that holds everything together. If a shell or bone is encased in such a rock, then the percolating fluids may deposit minerals in any holes, cavities or spaces. A specimen is often said to be *petrified* in this case, that is, it has been turned into stone.

An alternative result may involve the fossil being removed by percolating solutions, particularly if the solution is acidic. The hard part is then partially or totally replaced by later solutions depositing (i.e. filling in with) minerals in the cavity that has been formed. Another possibility is that when the shell or bone has been dissolved and removed, a cavity remains and the hollow mould is then found by the palaeontologist.

There are many other types of fossil in addition to shells, bones and similar hard types of skeleton. Trace fossils are commonly found, and these record the presence or activity of an organism. A good example is a footprint of an animal. If a creature walks on soft mud, an impression or print will be left. If this dries a little, just enough to retain its shape, and is then covered by fresh sediment, particularly of a different type (say sand), then it is likely that an infilling of that impression will be preserved. Trace fossils are more common where different types of sediment meet because the differences in the type of rock subsequently formed help preserve the fossil. Other examples of trace fossils include burrows, tubes, tooth or claw marks. Eggs are also considered to be trace fossils, as are fossil excreta (excrement), which are called *coprolites*.

Fossilised plants can be found as replicas of the

original, either preserved by sediment or by a thin organic film on the rock. Plants are frequently found as fossils in shale bands within a mainly sandstone sequence of rocks. However, if the sandstone has fine grains, then it may also yield fossils.

Plant fossils may also be discovered as a thin black trace on the surface of the rock when it is split open. This is an organic film (that is, composed of carbon or compounds of carbon) that has been created by the weight and pressure of the accumulating sediments above. The original plant material loses most, if not all, of its other elements to leave this black film. This process of pressure and change is called *distillation*. Leaves and plants preserved in this way often show a great deal of detail.

In exceptional circumstances, plant fossils have been found that still retain a trace of green colour, caused by the original green-coloured chlorophyll that is found in living plants. However, the amateur collector is unlikely to make such an uncommon find. The most common fossil from the plant world is pollen, because it has a very hard outer case that prevents breakdown. The study of pollen is a science in its own right, called *palynology*.

There are other exceptional ways in which organisms and animals can be preserved, but, again, the casual collector is unlikely to come across them. These include the entrapment of insects in tree resin (called amber when it hardens), the deep-freezing of mammoths in thick ice and the preservation of humans in acidic bogs. These last two examples are not really considered fossils as they are relatively recent when compared to the majority of organisms found in the fossil record.

It must be remembered when collecting and studying fossils that the picture that can be built from fossils is an incomplete one. From what has already been said, it becomes clear that hard parts are preserved more easily than soft tissues so there is a bias in favour of organisms with a skeleton—either internal or external (i.e. a shell). You are much more likely to find a fossil shell than a fossil jellyfish!

Even with all these drawbacks, fossils do contribute to the evolutionary record, in many instances providing remarkable detail. Some experts would say fossils add to the record of macroevolution, which is the development of organisms above the level of species. An example of this would be the evolution of mammals from reptiles.

These sorts of theories are fine but have little direct impact, at least at this stage, on the collection of fossil shells from local rocks. However, what is important is the distribution of fossils in rocks of various ages and the particuar rock types that occurred over time.

PART THREE

AGES, ROCKS AND STRATIGRAPHY

The Earth is very old: current estimates based on the dating of rocks estimate that it is just over four and a half billion years old—that is 4600 million years! Dating methods in geology rely on radioactive elements that break down through the release of minute radioactive particles over a very long period of time. Scientists (*geochronologists*) can measure the ratio of such an element to its breakdown products and then estimate the age of a particular rock. Different elements break down over different time periods. By using these methods and the way in which different rocks are placed next to each other, it has been possible to build up the *succession* (that is, the order in which the rocks were laid down) over geological time. Fossils have helped, because where the rock strata have not been disturbed too much by earth movements, they help to match one area with another and to identify any levels that are missing.

Of all the rock types that you may find in the countryside, *sedimentary* rocks are where fossils will be found. Sediments—mud, sand, silt and so on—make sedimentary rocks when they are fully compacted and hardened. Sedimentary rocks account for a very large proportion of the geological record, as we shall see.

There are two other major groups or types of rocks. These are *igneous* and *metamorphic* rocks. Igneous rocks are formed deep in the Earth as molten material, obviously at very high temperatures. This material then either cools slowly beneath the surface or is pushed into other rocks as sheets, or it may be poured out onto the surface in a volcanic eruption. Because these rocks start at very high temperatures, there is clearly no chance of fossils being preserved, even if an organism were to come into contact with the rock. The final group of rocks is called *metamorphic* rocks. These are formed from any other existing rock that, because of the action of great pressure or heat, or both, changes its form and make-up. It is possible to find fossils in sedimentary rocks that have then been altered (or metamorphosed) in this way, providing the metamorphism has not been too severe. For example, some trilobites (*see* page 50) have been found squashed into different shapes because of this effect. If the metamorphic processes are intense, the original rock changes a great deal, with the growth of new minerals usually at a different orientation from those in the original rock, and fossils are therefore either destroyed or rendered almost unrecognisable.

Turning our attention to sedimentary rocks, we need to look at the way in which the geological record has been divided. There are three major divisions of the geological timescale, called *eons* and they are named:

Archaean—the oldest division from which no traces of life are found.

Proterozoic—from which only very simple organisms are found, consisting in the main of just one cell.

Phanerozoic—the youngest division, which began around 600 million years ago and in which the vast array of plant and animal life flourished.

The Phanerozoic is then divided further into eras. The oldest is the *Palaeozoic*, which lasted from 600 to 248 million years ago (mya), during which most of the major plant and animal groups appeared. From 248 to 64 mya was the *Mesozoic* era. This was the time of the dinosaurs and also saw the development of many groups that had the features that we see today. The final era, the *Cenozoic*, began 64 mya and is with us still. During this time, mammals have become a dominant land life-form and flowering plants have developed enormously from their origin in the Mesozoic.

These eras are then further subdivided into periods, and it is this division that forms the core of our study. *Stratigraphy* is the name given to the branch of geology that deals with stratified rocks (i.e. rocks, sediment, that were laid down in sheet-like beds) in terms of time and space. Figure 1 gives a simplified version.

Throughout the periods listed, apart from the Precambrian, sedimentary rocks have dominated, although there have been numerous events involving

Figure 1: A basic geologic timescale

ERA	PERIOD	EPOCH	AGE (millions of years since the start)
	Quaternary	Recent or Holocene	0.01
		Pleistocene	2
CENOZOIC		Pliocene	5
		Miocene	25
	Tertiary	Oligocene	38
		Eocene	55
		Palaeocene	65
	Cretaceous		144
MESOZOIC	Jurassic		213
	Triassic		248
	Permian		286
	Carboniferous		360
PALAEOZOIC	Devonian		408
	Silurian		438
	Ordovician		505
	Cambrian		590
	PRECAMBRIAN		to 4600

metamorphism and igneous activity. Beginning with the Cambrian, we can now take a brief look at the distinctive rock types that were formed and the commoner types of creatures that were found. The different organisms mentioned will be dealt with later.

Cambrian

Cambrian rocks were first studied in Wales, and this is the origin of the name (from *Cambria*, the Latin for Wales). It was dominantly a marine environment, i.e. sediments laid down in the sea, producing sands and silts. There are not many places where Cambrian rocks are found in the UK, notably Wales and northwest Scotland and the Midlands. Sandy strata have now been compacted into quartzites (hard, quartz-rich rocks, quartz being the mineral that makes up sand). There are many shales, sandy flagstones and also some limestones. Figure 2 shows, approximately, the distribution of most of the major divisions and periods in the UK.

In these early seas, the common organisms were brachiopods, trilobites, molluscs, graptolites, crinoids, ostracods, radiolaria and foraminifera. This period marks the point at which fossils first become abundant. The trilobites were sufficiently common to enable geologists to create divisions or zones based on the fossil remains.

Ordovician

The Ordovician period takes its name from a Celtic tribe of north Wales, the Ordovices. Rocks of this age are found mainly in Wales, northwest England and the Southern Uplands of Scotland. There is a tremendous source of fossils in these rocks, which are commonly shales and slates with limestones and sandstones in places. In this period there was considerable volcanic activity, producing lavas, ashes and similar rock types. In some areas, such as the Lake District, these volcanic rocks are present rather than the sedimentary rocks. Where sedimentary rocks were deposited, many have been altered and moved by later geological processes so that fossils are not easily found.

The dominant fossils found are graptolites and trilobites. Graptolites have been used to identify zones in the Ordovician, and in many cases these organisms have been preserved in iron pyrites (iron sulphide, FeS_2, also called fool's gold). Brachiopods are not uncommon, and ostracods may also be found, as may echinoderms.

Silurian

This is yet another period that was named after a Welsh tribe, this time the Silures from the Welsh borders. This indicates how much activity there was in Wales and, indeed, the whole of the UK during the early days of geology. In many cases, the succession established in Britain became the standard by which other areas were studied and to which they were compared.

In the UK, rocks of Silurian age are found in the Welsh borders, northwest England, southern Scotland and parts of Ireland. Earth movements have resulted in the full sequence of rocks being missing in some areas, but it remains a very productive period for fossils.

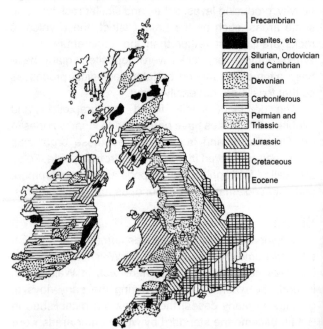

Figure 2: Distribution of rocks in the UK and Ireland

☐	Precambrian
■	Granites, etc
▨	Silurian, Ordovician and Cambrian
▦	Devonian
☰	Carboniferous
▨	Permian and Triassic
▨	Jurassic
▦	Cretaceous
▥	Eocene

Common to this period are thick mudstones, shales and slates, all deposited in seas of varying depth. There are also many massive limestones forming features on the countryside, and in northern England there are flag-stones and coarse sandstones. These all indicate the deposition of sediments in shallow seas.

Silurian fossils are dominated by graptolites, which again were used to zone all divisions of this period and are also often preserved in iron pyrites. Trilobites too were common and were joined by brachiopods, echinoderms and certain corals, which occurred in the earliest known coral reefs. There are many localities with limestone outcrops (that is, rocks that appear at the surface) that are rich in shelly fossils (brachiopods and molluscs). The Silurian is also the time during which the land became colonised by plants.

The Caledonian Orogeny, a massive mountain-building period of time, began in the late Silurian and continued into the next period, the Devonian.

Devonian

The conditions in the Devonian period were quite different from the environments that had gone before. The name is derived from Devon, where there are considerable deposits of Devonian age. These rocks are also found in south and mid-Wales, southern Scotland and on the northeastern coast of Scotland.

The dominant rock type is red sandstone, which gives a very distinctive colour to soils in these areas. There are two aspects to the Devonian based on rock type and therefore the conditions in which the rocks were laid down. Marine sediments, including sandstones, shales, limestones and mudstones, were deposited at the same time as continental deposits (that is, laid down on land), which were characterised by conglomerates (rocks made up of weathered, rounded fragments of other rocks) and the well-known Old Red Sandstone.

Because of this split in environment, the fossils to be found also differ. In the marine sequences are found corals, brachiopods, trilobites and goniatites, while the Old Red Sandstone is known for plant and fish remains.

Carboniferous

The Carboniferous period derives its name from the presence of large volumes of coal-bearing rocks. However, it contains a tremendous variety of rock types and in all reaches a considerable thickness. In the USA it is so thick that it has been divided into two separate systems. In the UK, Carboniferous rocks cover very large areas of central and northern Britain, running along the spine of the country. Southern Scotland also has considerable outcrops, and the whole of Ireland has extensive coverage (*see* figure 2).

The Carboniferous period in Britain may be divided loosely into three parts: Carboniferous Limestone (Lower Carboniferous), Millstone Grit and Coal Measures (mainly Upper Carboniferous). These are obviously divisions based on the dominant rock type. The early part of this period was characterised by warm, shallow seas in which limestones and sandstones were formed. The Millstone Grit consists of coarse sandstones with some shales, indicating deposition in shallow water and deltas (that is, where a river flows into the sea and a lot of sediment is laid down). The Coal Measures are essentially representative of deltas, swamps and other environments at the edge of the land. The rock types are very mixed, with sandstones, shales, limestones and oil shales, among which are found coal seams.

The variety of fossils reflects environmental changes and depositional conditions. In the Lower Carboniferous are found brachiopods, crinoids, fish fragments, bryozoans and goniatites. The Millstone Grit contains goniatites (in the shales), and while the coarse sandy sediments are not ideal for fossils, plant remains may be found. The Coal Measures contain many plant remains, including mosses and ferns, bark and roots. There is a diverse selection such as brachiopods, bivalves (molluscs), corals and crinoids, goniatites, fish remains and even the more exotic dragonfly.

At the end of the Carboniferous there were further earth movements, which led to non-marine conditions for a considerable length of time.

Permian

The Permian period takes its name from Permia, a kingdom of the past, located between the Urals and the

Volga. Conditions were arid or semi-arid and led to the deposition of sandstones and marls (calcareous clays often deposited in lakes) and some limestones. The distribution of Permian rocks in Britain is quite limited, occurring mainly down the central spine of central and northern England, southwest and northern England and in small areas of southern Scotland.

Fossils are not very common in Permian strata, but there are some brachiopods, bivalves and fishes. There are also some places where plants may be found.

Triassic

This is the first period of the Mesozoic era, and it derives its name from the threefold division in Germany. In Britain these rocks are found in a ribbon running in a roughly diagonal line from the south coast near Lyme Regis to the north Yorkshire coast just north of Whitby. Then a large offshoot extends from the Midlands around Birmingham and Stafford, northwest to the Lancashire coast. There are scattered outcrops elsewhere, around the Solway Firth, but little more.

Rocks from this era were laid down primarily on the land or in lakes and therefore consist of sandstones, conglomerates and marls. Because of the high salt content of lake waters, animal life was poor. Until the late Triassic, therefore, little was preserved save for some skeletal debris from fishes, amphibians and reptiles.

However, the late Triassic saw a change in conditions to shallow seas, thereby producing limestones with some brachiopods. There are occasional bone beds, which consist predominantly of fish skeletal remains.

Jurassic

The Jurassic period, named after the Jura Mountains in France, witnessed a deepening of the sea, the connecting of previously isolated bodies of water and an abundance of life. Typical rock types include great thicknesses of limestone, with shales, marls and also sandstones and clays. Jurassic rocks occur in a band running diagonally southwest to northeast across England, lying to the southeast of the Triassic (*see* figure 2).

Some exposures of rocks are absolutely full of fossils, and one dominant fossil form is the ammonite, which has been used to zone the Jurassic based on the many species found. Belemnites are also found in the marls, as are crinoids. The Lower Jurassic has also yielded more exotic remains in the form of ichthyosaurs and plesiosaurs, both marine reptiles, but teeth or other small items such as vertebrae are more common.

Brachiopods, bivalves, sea urchins, corals and ammonites are found in the Inferior Oolite, a particular type of limestone, and fossil plants are common in some beds of a deltaic or estuarine origin (i.e. in the mouth of a river). This rich collection of fossils continues up the

Jurassic, with a tremendous variety of shells and also vertebrates being found.

Of course, the Jurassic was the era of the dinosaurs, although fossils of this group are more common in the next period. However, plants are found from the Jurassic, including ferns, conifers and a palm-like bush.

Cretaceous

The Cretaceous period is named after the chalk (creta) by which it is well known. Considerable areas of England are covered with rocks of this age, lying in outcrop to the east of the Jurassic and found over the southeast, much of East Anglia and also on the east coast a little farther north.

The Cretaceous began in the south with a continuation of the non-marine conditions of the late Jurassic, producing sandstones and clays with few fossils save for well-known remains of reptiles and fossil tree trunks. Farther north the sea invaded, and eventually these conditions reached the south and deposited sandstones with clays that often have an abundance of ammonites, brachiopods and gastropods. Conditions then changed again, with a much higher lime content that led to the formation of substantial thicknesses of chalk with limestones. It contains ammonites, bivalves, echinoids, belemnites and also sharks' teeth.

Dinosaurs remained dominant during the Cretaceous

and fishes were common, but at the end of the period, about 65 mya, the dinosaurs became extinct.

Tertiary

The Tertiary contains much of the last 60 million years or so of the Earth's history. In Britain, rocks of this age are mainly in the south and southeast of England, around London, Norfolk, Southampton and the Isle of Wight.

The rocks found include sands, clays and shelly sands of mixed marine and non-marine origin. There are also deposits formed by rivers. The fossils in the Tertiary are mainly bivalves and gastropods, with fish, reptile and mammal remains such as vertebrae, teeth and scales.

Quaternary

The most recent geological period is the Quaternary, which includes the present. It began around two million years ago and during that time there have been several glaciations and mammals continued their growth to become the dominant land life-form.

PART FOUR

FINDING AND COLLECTING FOSSILS

Fossil collecting can be undertaken at various levels. It may be an occasional pastime or a hobby that takes every bit of your spare time. Whichever is the case, it is important that you are well prepared with the correct equipment, and it helps to plan ahead and find whatever information you can about your own area or the area you are to visit.

WHERE TO LOOK FOR FOSSILS

A good place to start is in sedimentary rocks and any exposure or outcrop of rocks in which you can see the bedding or strata as flat, parallel layers. This means that the best places are the coast, where often enormous stretches of cliff provide easy access. The banks of rivers and streams, road cuttings, hill tops, quarries are all likely sites of interest.

WARNING

Many of the potential sites for fossil hunting could be dangerous places. Younger collectors should therefore be accompanied by adults on such expeditions.

It may also be that the land where the rock outcrops are situated is private. It is important that permission be sought to gain access to the land and the rocks. In some cases, safety regulations may deny access to a site.

Project

Finding geological information

It is better, and usually leads to a more successful expedition, if you study the local geology before setting out. There are many sources of information that will show where the rocks are to be found, what they are, and whether they are fossiliferous (that Is, contain fossils). Geological maps produced by the Geological Survey provide a lot of information on the distribution of rocks in a particular area. There are also guides, some published also by the Geological Survey and others from local geological associations. This last type often provides specific walks or tours that show some interesting geological features and indicate what fossils are to be found and where. In addition, if a local university or college has a department of geology, it will almost certainly have maps, books and experts available and probably its own collection of rocks and fossils. It is always worth looking at real samples, so that when out on an expedition, you have some idea of what you are looking at and looking for. Museums are another source of samples and displays. Finally, there are many books on the subject of palaeontology, which the keener collector may wish to buy.

EQUIPMENT FOR FOSSIL COLLECTING

If you have the correct eqipment, the task of collection will be made much easier. In a particularly fossil-rich rock, perhaps where the surface of the bedding has been exposed by weathering, it may be possible simply to observe the fossils where they are. However, collection is quite a different matter, and there are certain tools that really are essential.

It is equally important that you are clothed properly. Strong, hard-wearing outer garments will shield you from the weather and cushion you when lying on cold stone in awkward positions! A pair of strong, waterproof boots will help you scramble over rocks and give some protection to your toes should a rock or boulder fall onto your foot. Similarly, for protection, it is vital to wear a hard hat, such as those worn by workmen on a building site.

Figure 3 shows some more items that are necessary. These are:

hammer—it is preferable to have a geological hammer, or two. These hammers are specially made for chipping specimens out of rocks and some have specially shaped blades. A lighter one is useful for more delicate work while a heavy one is suitable for breaking harder rock or for use with a chisel. There are several companies that deal with the supply of geological equipment.

chisel—a cold chisel is very useful for splitting larger pieces of rock or for separating the smaller laminations

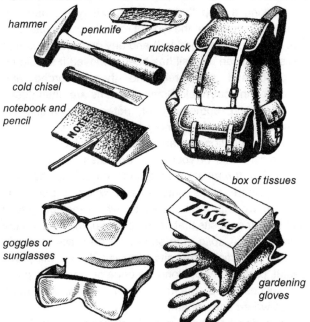

Figure 3: Some items of equipment of use when collecting fossils

hammer

penknife

rucksack

cold chisel

notebook and pencil

box of tissues

goggles or sunglasses

gardening gloves

(small scale bedding) to reveal fossils. It is recommended that you have two sizes. A standard hardware or tool shop will have something suitable.

notebook and pencil—it is important to record details of the specimens that you are collecting. At each location you should ideally make a note of exactly where you are on the map, either by noting down the grid reference or by marking a map that you have with you. Then you should add details of the type of rock, its colour, bedding (i.e. thickly or thinly bedded) and any other features that are seen. When a fossil has been removed it should be wrapped and numbered and then recorded and described in your book. Small diagrams are often useful for recording something of note, or perhaps an interesting fossil that cannot be reached or collected.

map—as mentioned earlier, it is possible to obtain geological maps of your area, and these come in two forms. A *drift map* shows the surface geology, that is, it shows where rocks outcrop and where the rock is covered by superficial deposits, which include glacial and similar deposits that have been laid down during the Quaternary. A *solid map* shows all the rocks at depth, with all superficial deposits removed. Either will prove useful, particularly as along the edge of the map is given the succession of the rocks for the area, with fossil zones where appropriate.

In addition to these geological maps, an Ordnance Survey map is very helpful. These are available at a variety of scales, and one that shows the details of an area—roads, lanes, buildings and so on—will allow you to pinpoint your location. Indeed, collecting sites can be numbered on the map and then used in your notebook.

If the weather looks at all doubtful, it need not restrict

your plans but it will aid your work if the maps and notebook are kept under plastic or in a polythene bag. If they are fastened to a board, and the bag is large enough, then notes can be made, even in the rain.

rucksack—you will realise that there are quite a few items of equipment to carry, so a rucksack or something similar is indispensible. In addition, when returning from a site, you will probably have lumps of rock containing fossils to carry. Finally, if you are out for some time, you will probably want to take a packed lunch—something not to be overlooked!

sample bags—when a sample has been removed, it should be wrapped, numbered and put in a bag for taking away. Newspaper will do if nothing else is available.

protective gear—in addition to the boots and outer garments, it is very important that eyes and hands are protected. When chipping away at a rock, particularly a hard limestone, for example, chips of stone may easily become dislodged and fly out at speed. It is very easy for eyes to be damaged so it is vital to wear eye protection. Goggles are ideal but glasses or sunglasses do afford some protection.

Similarly for hands—a hammer can easily miss or glance off a chisel and fingers can at least be bruised if not broken. A pair of good, strong gloves is therefore an essential part of your equipment. Some types of gardening gloves are suitable in this respect.

hand lens—a hand lens or magnifying glass is worth carrying, although not essential. It does allow you to study a feature on a fossil in more detail or to magnify a small fossil, e.g. a graptolite. Standard geological hand lenses provide a magnification of 10, and the lens part conveniently hinges out from a metal case. They also can be obtained from geological supply shops.

Finally, certain extras never go amiss, such as marker pens, a small cloth and, of course, a camera, which can prove very useful in several ways. It allows you to record the larger details, such as the general appearance of an outcrop, and the finer points, such as the fossil in place before removal, or another fossil that is out of reach or unobtainable but worth noting.

Project

Collecting

When a suitable outcrop has been found, look at it all carefully, unless it is a cliff section, in which case look around a small area initially. There is no point attacking the rock face with your hammer—you will either destroy the fossils you have come to find or splinters of rock will go flying in all directions.

Assess the type of rock and look for points of weakness into which a chisel or hammer can be introduced to remove a piece. Look around to see if weathering and erosion have exposed fossils, or particular levels with fossils that may be explored further along the outcrop. Then, using your hammer and chisel, break off a lump of rock or split it apart in the hope of finding a fossil. Be careful not to drive your chisel too far into a crack or it may become jammed. When a fossil has been found, if it is still in position, make a note of it and take a photograph.

As the fossil is removed, try not to break it. A brachiopod in a massive limestone will probably withstand a lot of hammering, but a trilobite or graptolite on shale will be more likely to break or crack. It is perfectly acceptable to remove the fossil and the surrounding piece of rock rather than trying to chip the waste rock away and, in so doing, damaging the fossil.

After removal, wrap and bag the fossil. After completing your notes, label it and put it in your rucksack. If you find a fossil that is very large or unusual, it is better to leave it where it is, take a photograph and call in an expert from the local museum or university geology department. Many's the time that an over-enthusiastic amateur has ruined a good fossil, and in any case a large fossil such as a dinosaur skeleton needs great expertise and also a lot of helpers and time if it is to be removed. Your photograph will establish who got there first!

After your day out, the fossils can be dealt with at home. It may be possible to remove a fossil completely from the surrounding rock, but in many cases it will have to be left where it is. In any event, the sample can be cleaned carefully, identified properly and labelled. Small display boxes can be made quite easily if you want to have a proper display that grows over the years. It is also useful for permanent storage to buy or make a simple cabinet with drawers. Figures 4a and 4b show some readily made examples for small or larger fossils.

Project

A simple cabinet

The simplest way to make a cabinet is to collect empty matchboxes. When you have enough, glue them together in rows, one row on top of the next. This makes a cabinet complete with individual drawers, each of which can be labelled with its contents (figure 4a). Leave the back of the cabinet open so that you can easily open a drawer by pushing it from the back with a finger. You do not need handles on each drawer.

If you want a more finished looking job, cover over the sides, bottom and top of the matchbox cabinet with pieces of sheet balsa cut to fit (figure 4b). You can cover in the back with balsa sheet or a piece of hardboard glued in place. You will need to fit a handle to each drawer. This can be a short length of hardwood dowel stuck to the front of each door with balsa cement. You can make specimen cabinets of any size this way, simply

Figure 4a: An easy way of storing small fossils

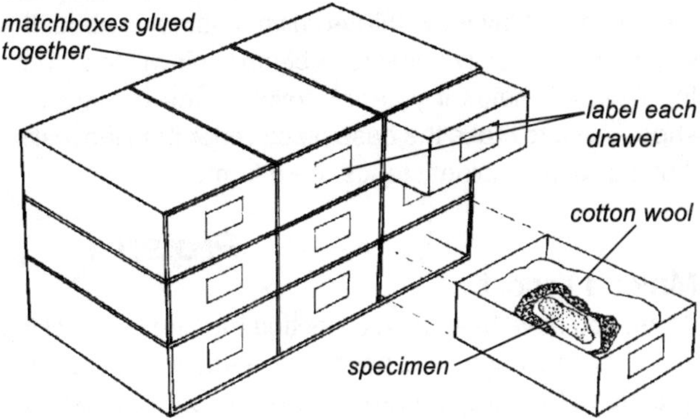

matchboxes glued together

label each drawer

cotton wool

specimen

Figure 4b

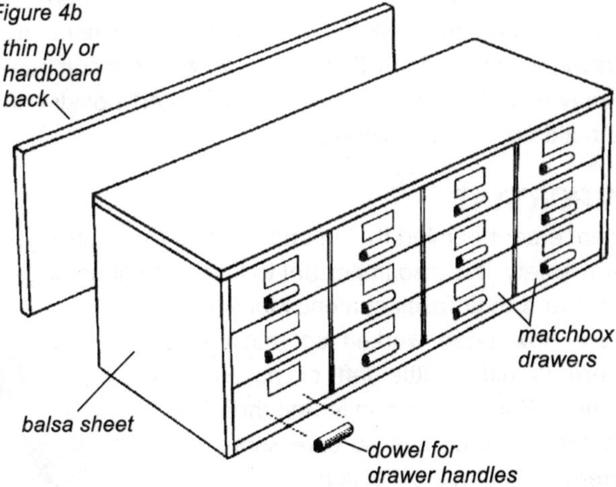

thin ply or hardboard back

matchbox drawers

balsa sheet

dowel for drawer handles

adding to the number of matchboxes in each layer and the number of layers. A thirty-drawer cabinet is about the largest that is really suitable. A bigger unit will tend to be top heavy. It helps if you are covering the cabinet with sheet balsa to make the base piece wider than the rest so that the whole cabinet stands more firmly.

Project

Make a report

When you have been on a collecting trip and by checking in books, museums, etc, have identified your fossils, it's a good idea to prepare a report. This can consist of a map showing the overall site and its location, where the fossils came from at the site, with descriptions and drawings of your finds. If you have access to a computer, it may even be possible to create a 'printed' booklet and to build up your own library.

IMPORTANT

Please bear in mind that in addition to looking after your own safety, it is also important to take care of geological sites and their fossil content. Many sites have now been worked so much that there is either little left or access is denied. Fossils are a finite and therefore limited resource and so care should be exercised in their collection.

PART FIVE

INVERTEBRATE FOSSIL GROUPS

We shall now look at the more important groups of fossils, their general appearance and illustrate some typical examples that you may find in your collecting. These are merely an indication and a small selection from the vast number of fossil species that have been identified but it will point you in the right direction. Do refer to other comprehensive books and museum collections to aid your identification.

You will note that all fossils, as indeed with all animals, are given a double-barrelled name such as the trilobite *Dalmanites myops*. This is a Latin name that is unique to the individual organism. The first part indicates the genus and the second part is the species. Within each genus there may be a number of species, all with some features in common. The examples quoted here are in the main identified only by their genus.

Foraminifera

Known as forams for short, these are a fossil group that you are unlikely to meet but it is worth a brief mention. Ninety per cent of all forams identified are from the fossil record, and they are very important components of sedimentary rocks, especially chalk. The difficulty is that a microscope is necessary to see most of them, although some reach half a millimetre, which would be visible with a hand lens. The body chamber is made of chalk, silica (i.e. the same chemical composition as sand) or sand grains, and the shape may be a sphere, a tube or some sort of spiral.

Foraminifera (which belong to the kingdom Protista in zoological classification) have been and are so common that, with similar organisms, they cover thousands of square miles of ocean floor and have made sediments of enormous thicknesses. Figure 5 shows some of the general shape of foram body chambers.

Figure 5: Some Foraminifera chamber shapes

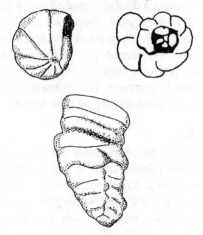

Sponges

Sponges belong to the phylum *Porifera* (meaning 'pore bearers') and are a simple form of multicellular organism. The walls of a sponge have two layers of cells in which there are pores. Water is drawn in through the pores into a central cavity, called the spongocoel, and then flows out through an opening (the occulum) at the 'top' of the organism. In this process, food particles in the water are collected. The base of the sponge is fixed to a rock and the body shape is very variable. The support for the body is provided by spicules, which are needle-like pieces of chalk or silica and are a common form of microfossil. Figure 6 illustrates the general structure of a sponge.

Sponges are found in the fossil record from the Cambrian onwards, and figure 7 on page 42 gives some examples from the Cretaceous, which are found mainly in the chalk.

Figure 6: General structure of a sponge

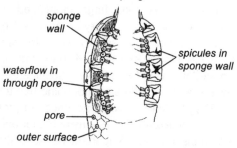

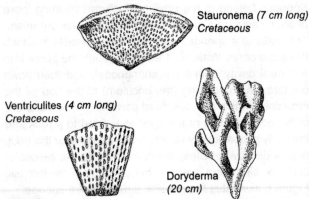

Figure 7: Examples of sponges

Stauronema *(7 cm long)*
Cretaceous

Ventriculites *(4 cm long)*
Cretaceous

Doryderma
(20 cm)

Corals

Corals form one group of coelenterates or, as modern classifiction would have it, the phylum *Cnidaria*. Others in the phylum include the anemones and jelly fish. The corals (also called anthozoans) live in the sea and are colonial, that is, they form large interlinked masses rather than living alone as solitary organisms. However, there are some solitary forms. They live on the bottom of the sea and have tough skeletons of chalk, lime or horny organic material. Living forms have a sac-like body with a two-layered wall and the single opening has a ring of tentacles. They typically have no advanced organs such as the nervous or excretory systems of higher animals.

Fossil corals are very important because they are

effectively rock-builders. In the warm oceans where temperatures were high (21°C/70°F or more) and the waters were clean, coral reefs grew to very great thicknesses. On dying, individual members (or polyps) of a colony would leave behind their calcareous skeletons, and over time these would build up and consolidate to form a massive limestone reef. The individual cups containing a polyp preserve well, and this group, in its colonial form, is found in the Ordovician. The individual non-colonial forms existed long before then. Reefs are very widely distributed in the geological record and their location now is an indication of how the climate has changed with time. In some cases, they are important in oil exploration because they form reservoirs which hold the oil after it has formed from organic matter. The basic form of a solitary coral is shown in figure 8.

Figure 8: The basic fossil coral shape

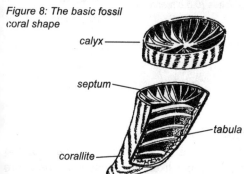

calyx

septum

tabula

corallite

The fossil group has a number of divisions, depending on shape, the absence or presence of certain features, e.g. septa, or whether they were solitary or colonial. Figure 9 shows some typical examples: *Halysites*, a chain-like coral made up of branching rows of thin corals, which comes from the Silurian to Devonian; a Carboniferous colonial coral *Lithostrotion*, which had strong septa and corallite (*see* figure 8 for the terms) edges; and *Syringopora*, from the Silurian to Carboniferous, which is a colonial form with separate corallites (i.e. individual coral 'tubes') that are connected by cross branches.

Figure 9: Fossil corals

Halysites *(0.5 cm across)*

Lithostrotion

Syringopora *(3 cm across)*

Brachiopods

Brachiopods form one of the fossil groups that the palaeontologist is most likely to encounter. There are about 30,000 species known from the Palaeozoic and Mesozoic, but only 1 per cent of this number exist today. The peak for brachiopods was in the Palaeozoic, but at the end of the Permian period their numbers fell away quite dramatically and that remains the situation today.

Otherwise known as lamp shells, brachiopods are marine organisms that attach themselves to the sea bed by a short stalk or *pedicle*. Most attached themselves to rock, but some were partially burrowing and lived in a tube-like hole with a longer pedicle anchored at the bottom of the hole. The shell is made up of two parts (or valves), and although brachiopods resemble the bivalves (*see* page 47), the latter have valves that are usually the same. The line of symmetry (an imaginary line that can be drawn, about which the two halves are the same) in bivalves is along the hinge whereas in brachiopods it is down the shell (*see* figure 10).

The shell, of course, protects the soft body parts within, which lie at the back towards the hinge. There are

Figure 10: Comparison of symmetry between brachiopods (left) and bivalve (right). The line indicates the plane of symmetry

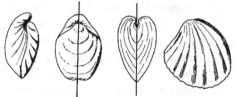

two types of hinge producing a division of the group into *articulate* and *inarticulate*. Inarticulate brachiopods had valves made of calcium phosphate and chitin held together by muscles. The much larger articulate group had shells made of lime, and the two valves were held together by muscles but also by interlocking teeth. These can be seen on shells today. The bulk of the space in the shell was taken up by an organ called the *lophophore*, which was a circular fold-like structure that had tentacles with cilia (tiny hair-like extensions). The cilia draw water to the mouth and, with it, food particles. The lophophore therefore acts as a sieving mechanism when the shell is open.

Most brachiopods are between 1 and 5 centimetres in length or width, and the shape of the valves, the hinge structure and the internal marks where muscles were attached (for closing the shell) are all useful in identifying species. Brachiopods were adaptable and widespread, and different forms would live in different parts of the marine habitat.

Figure 11 shows some fossil brachiopods. *Spirifer* was a Carboniferous form and is typical of a group that was common at that time. It has a characteristically triangular outline and a wide hinge with a sort of fold down the centre of the valve. *Lingula* is an example of an inarticulate brachiopod and is very unusual in that it is one of the longest-lived organisms, being found first in

Figure 11: Fossil brachiopods (measurements are all widths)

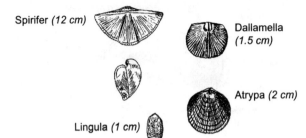

Spirifer *(12 cm)*

Dallamella *(1.5 cm)*

Atrypa *(2 cm)*

Lingula *(1 cm)*

the Cambrian and yet it can still be found today. *Dalmanella*, from the Ordovician and Lower Silurian, is a small form with a roughly circular outline. It shows fine ribs and growth lines. Finally, *Atrypa* (mid-Silurian to Devonian) is a common form with a flatter pedicle (or ventral) valve and convex brachial valve.

Bivalves

The bivalves (class *Bivalvia* or *Pelecypoda*) are one group of molluscs. Other examples of molluscs are snails and octopuses, but the bivalves include clams, oysters, mussels and scallops. In outward appearance, bivalves resemble brachiopods but their symmetry (*see* figure 10) and other factors—internal organs, composition of the shell—set them apart.

The two valves of a bivalve are therefore usually

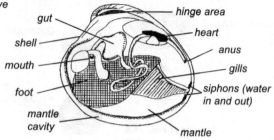

Figure 12: Diagrammatic representation of the main organs in a bivalve

Labels: hinge area, gut, heart, shell, anus, mouth, gills, foot, siphons (water in and out), mantle cavity, mantle

similar and are joined along the hinge line and held together by muscles (called adductor muscles) and interlocking teeth on the hinge itself. Most bivalves are marine, but some live in fresh water. Some are attached to the surface or lie on the surface of the sea bed, while others use their foot to burrow. The foot can also be used to move along the sea bed. The mantle cavity, i.e. the space in the shell, contains the soft parts and organs such as the gills (used for feeding and exchange of gases), heart, gut, foot, mouth and anus. Figure 12 shows the main organs of a bivalve. Food particles are carried in on water currents generated by the siphon, and these particles are then trapped on the gills.

In the fossil record, bivalves are very common and from the Palaeozoic onwards are abundant. The composition of the shell, protein with calcite or aragonite (both forms of calcium carbonate), renders it very tough and easily preserved. Because many species live in shallow water, they give some indication of the location of ancient shorelines.

Figure 13 illustrates a number of fossil bivalves. *Modiolopsis* was found in the Ordovician and Silurian and reached a maximum length of 4 centimetres. It is found in Shropshire. *Carbonicola*, as its name suggests, is a Carboniferous bivalve, from the Coal Measures, and was a freshwater form. It often has thick, concentric growth lines. *Nucula* is interesting and is often called a living fossil, having shown little or no change since the Silurian. *Trigonia* is a Mesozoic bivalve of distinctive

Figure 13: Some fossil bivalves

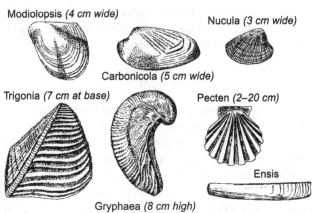

Modiolopsis *(4 cm wide)*

Nucula *(3 cm wide)*

Carbonicola *(5 cm wide)*

Trigonia *(7 cm at base)*

Pecten *(2–20 cm)*

Ensis

Gryphaea *(8 cm high)*

shape and with a very strong pattern on the valves. Found from the Jurassic to the Recent, the valves have a pronounced ridge, and it can reach 9 centimetres in length. *Gryphaea* is a very well-known form that looks very little like a bivalve! Because of its unusual shape it is nicknamed the Devil's toenail and is common in rocks from the Jurassic to the Eocene. The two valves have grown quite asymmetrically so that the right valve is like a lid on the tightly coiled left valve. It is particularly common in the Lower Lias (Lower Jurassic). There are far too many bivalves to include here, but it is perhaps worth mentioning two that are seen today. *Pecten* is very distinctive and first appeared in the Lower Carboniferous. It has strong radial ribs and unequal wings along the hinge line. Finally, *Ensis* (Tertiary to Recent) is the common razor shell and is very elongated, reaching up to 25 centimetres in length. It occurs from the Tertiary to the Recent.

Trilobites

This is a fascinating group of fossil arthropods. The arthropods (which means 'jointed feet') have been and still are a very successful phylum within the animal kingdom. Around one million arthropod species have been described and roughly two-thirds of all known organisms are arthropods—that is, insects, crustaceans and spiders. Their success is due in great part to their hard outer skeleton (exoskeleton), the segmentation of their bodies and the jointed appendages (legs, mouth parts, etc). The segmentation of the body usually produces a three-fold division into the head, body and tail. The hard body wall cannot move, so when the animal grows too large, it sheds its skin and grows one that is larger.

Trilobites are an extinct group of marine arthropods and are commonly found in rocks of Cambrian to late Permian age. They have a long flat body, similar in shape to a woodlouse, which has ridges and furrows caused by the segmentation. The general form is shown in figure 14. These creatures commonly have a three-fold division lengthways into an axis and two pleural lobes and also across the body into a head part, the cephalon, which is specialised and then the thorax and pygidium. The cephalon is fused into a sort of shield and contains simple compound eyes. This part shows all

Figure 14: Basic structure of the trilobite

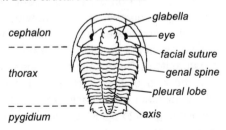

sorts of variations particularly in the length of the side spines. The thorax and pygidium are made up of segments that are essentially the same except that they gradually taper in width to the tail. Each of the segments had a jointed leg at either side. The average size of a trilobite was 2–10 centimetres, although some have been found that were considerably larger.

The trilobites were relatively complex creatures that could move easily and in different ways. Some seem to have walked on the tips of their legs, some 'waded' through the sea-floor mud, and others were good swimmers. In each case the appendages showed variations and adaptations. It seems they were scavengers, eating animal or vegetable remains that they found, and some forms seem to have preyed on smaller animals, including smaller trilobites. Some forms were blind and others were able to curl up into a ball, presumably as a means of protection.

At some point in the geological record, trilobites are very common, and often on a particular bedding plane within a shale, a great number of fossils may be found. It is more common to find pieces than a whole animal, and very often the fossil is the remains of a shed skin rather than the creature itself. There seems no reason for their extinction at the end of the Permian, but they faded away, as did many other marine animals.

Some trilobites grew to a considerable size, and one

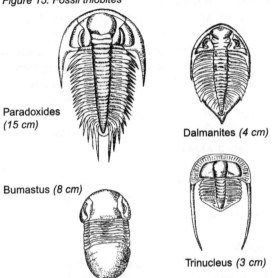

Figure 15: Fossil trilobites

Paradoxides *(15 cm)*

Dalmanites *(4 cm)*

Bumastus *(8 cm)*

Trinucleus *(3 cm)*

genus, *Paradoxides*, has been found 30 centimetres or more in length. This was a middle Cambrian form with a semicircular cephalon and a long thorax. *Dalmanites* is found from the Silurian to the Lower Devonian. It has a larger glabella and the eyes are raised above the surface of the cephalon. The eleven thoracic segments have spines. It is commonly 5–6 centimetres in length but can be more. *Trinucleus* (specific name *fimbriatus*) is a very well-known form from the Ordovician. It is characterised by a large cephalon, in comparison to the rest of the body, which has indentations around the rim. It also has long spines that commonly exceed the overall length of the body. *Calymene* has a furrowed glabella and also occurs in a rolled-up form (*Flexicalymene*). Another trilobite that is found rolled up is *Phacops*, and this often occurs with large compound eyes. A slightly unusual form with fewer segmentations is *Bumastus*, which is oval in outline. Found in the Ordovician and Silurian, it has a wide central lobe on the cephalon with no real development of a glabella. It also has a very wide central (axial) lobe down the middle of the body and the pygidium shows no segmentation at all. Figure 15 illustrates some of these forms.

Graptolites

The graptolites are an intriguing group of fossils and one about which perhaps the least is known. On the rock surface, their fossils look quite insignificant, appearing as no more than a scratch or a very fine saw blade. In some cases they look almost like branching plant stems, but the general opinion is that they are very distantly related to chordates, which, by definition, have some sort of stiff rod along the length of the organism.

The earliest forms of graptolite were colonial and formed branching structures, each branch containing cup-like structures (called thecae) in which the organisms lived. Figure 16 provides an interpretation of the structure, and the column running up the back of the colony may have contained living tissue linking together the organisms. It is thought that the individuals had tentacles and fed on planktonic material Over time, graptolites became less complex and many forms had just one strand of thecae. The column, or stolon, that linked the thecae together appears to have been made of chitin, a tough hydrocarbon containing nitrogen, which also forms the exoskeleton of many insects.

Graptolites were entirely marine and have proved very useful in dating and correlating (matching) rocks. They evolved quickly, are relatively widespread and quite specific. They are a good example of an index fossil. They are found first in rocks of Cambrian age, and existed up to the end of the Carboniferous.

A typical branched form is *Dictyonema*, which measured roughly 3–4 centimetres. *Clonograptus* is also

Figure 16: Possible graptolite structure with thecae branching off the main stem in which the organisms lived

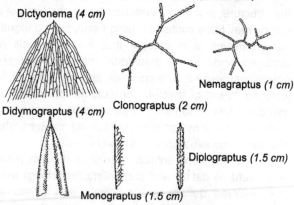

Figure 17: Fossil graptolites (all dimensions top to bottom)

Dictyonema *(4 cm)*

Nemagraptus *(1 cm)*

Didymograptus *(4 cm)* Clonograptus *(2 cm)*

Diplograptus *(1.5 cm)*

Monograptus *(1.5 cm)*

branched but in a different fashion. Both are found in rocks of Ordovician age. *Nemagraptus* is a widespread index fossil with S-shaped stems from which branches form offshoots. This is middle Ordovician in age and ranges in overall length up to 4 centimetres. It is more usual to find forms either with one or two branches, or to find sections of larger forms. *Didymograptus* is also an Ordovician form, and it consists of two branches (or stipes), found at varying angles.

A well-known solitary form from the Silurian is *Monograptus leintwardinensis*, which is found in the Ludlow series of Herefordshire. Mostly, graptolites are preserved in shales or shaly rocks where the fine-grained material retains the detail. *Diplograptus* is another Silurian form, with two rows of thecae back to back, which occurred quite commonly (*see* figure 17).

Gastropods

The gastropods are another mollusc group that has proved to be very successful. The class gastropoda contains over 40,000 species, and there are forms that live in sea water and fresh water, and some have also moved on to land. Most gastropods have a single shell that is twisted into a spiral and into which the animal can retreat. There is, however, an enormous variety in the form of the shells, which are calcareous in composition. The general form of the organism is shown in figure 18, but typical features are a muscular foot, with which they move, a head with tentacles and a very rough and abrasive tongue called the radula.

Figure 18: Simplified and schematic structure of a gastropod

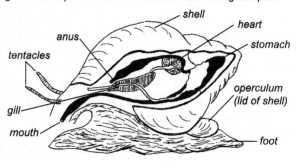

Figure 19: Fossil gastropods

Straparollus *(4 cm)*

Platyostoma *(4 cm)*

Torquesia *(3 cm)*

Planorbis *(1 cm)* with side view

Littorina *(2 cm)*

The classification of gastropods on their soft tissues—nervous system, gills and the radula—cannot be applied to fossil species. Palaeontologists therefore use the shape of the shell and, where possible, the chemical composition of the shell, as compared with modern forms.

Some forms of gastropod are found from the Cambrian, and early varieties mostly were marine. A typical individual from the Silurian to Devonian is *Platyostoma* (*see* figure 19), which has a flat low spiral form. This is related to a very loosely coiled example, *Platyceras* (Silurian to Permian). Both are about 3–4 centimetres in size. *Straparollus* is also found from the Silurian to the Permian and is another quite flatly coiled form. The centre of the shell is actually slightly indented

The other form of gastropod shell that is very familiar

is the elongated, twisted shape. A good example is *Torquesia* (also called *Turritella*), which can reach lengths of up to 10 centimetres. Other examples from the Cenozoic include quite ornamented varieties such as *Fusinus* (Cretaceous to Recent). *Planorbis* (Jurassic to Recent) is a freshwater species and is flatly coiled, reaching about 2 centimetres, and *Littorina* (Palaeocene to Recent) is readily recognised from beaches today.

Ammonites and belemnites

The ammonites were members of the class Cephalopoda, the most mobile of all the molluscs. Some modern members of the clan are extremely fast swimmers and can grow quite large, and this was also true of the ammonites. The general form of the soft tissue will have been similar to modern cephalopods, with tentacles and a funnel structure to create jets of water for movement. Ammonites possessed a strong external shell that was usually coiled. The animal lived in the last chamber, and previous chambers are divided by septa (singular, septum). In life, the smaller chambers would have been gas-filled to give buoyancy. Many ammonites are very well preserved, and they are used as index fossils.

The shell is very often patterned and is sometimes quite ornate, and this aids in identification. Ammonites are found from the Devonian to the end of the

Figure 20: Fossil ammonites.

detail of pattern on
Dactylioceras (6 cm)

Gastriocerus (6 cm
diameter)

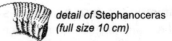

detail of Stephanoceras
(full size 10 cm)

Cretaceous when they suddenly became extinct. Figure 20 shows some examples. *Gastricoceras* is an Upper Carboniferous form with a typical indentation at the centre. It reached approximately 5 centimetres in diameter. Two lower Jurassic forms are *Hildoceras* (5–8 centimetres in diameter) and *Dactylioceras* (5–8 centimetres), both of which show very tight coils and considerable ribbing on the whorls (the coils). The septa that divide chambers in ammonites create very intricate lines where the septa edges meet the shell. These suture lines are often used in classifying ammonites, and the sutures of two species are shown in figure 21. *Stephanoceras* is a middle Jurassic form that has prominent ribs that branch at the middle of the whorl (*see* figure 20). It can reach up to 13 centimetres but is usually less.

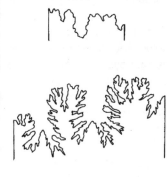

Figure 21: Two examples of ammonite sutures

Figure 22: A belemnite fossil, Belemnitella *(13 cm)*

Another cephalopod group distantly related to the ammonites is the belemnites. Their fossil remnants resemble bullets (*see* figure 22), and these were the internal skeleton or support to a squid-like animal. The fossil was in the centre of the animal, which was probably a fast swimmer. They are useful fossils in determining ages.

Crinoids and echinoids

The phylum *Echinodermata* contains a number of interesting groups and all 7000 members are marine. A common feature is radial symmetry, i.e. when a plane 'cutting' the animal in any direction gives equal and opposite halves or mirror images. In some groups the symmetry is five-fold, an uncommon feature in the animal kingdom.

Most forms are either fixed or very slow-moving and have a calcareous body skeleton. They move by a unique system, called the water vascular system, which is very well developed in echinoids (sea urchins). It consists of many water-filled tubes in a complex network that ends in numerous tube feet that protrude through the shell.

Crinoids are sea lilies, and these are organisms that have changed little in 500 million years. They consisted of a stem with a number of arms to which smaller fronds were attached (*see* figure 23). They are very common as fossils but usually only small pieces of the skeleton are found. Commonest are the plates that make up the stem.

Figure 23: Basic crinoid structure (left) and a Jurassic example, Pentacrinites *(5 cm)*

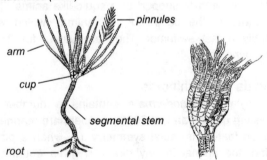

Crinoids were common in the Carboniferous although they first appeared in the Ordovician. *Pentacrinites* is an excellent example of a crinoid, unusually well preserved, and showing the structure clearly (figure 23).

Echinoids or sea urchins have tubercles covering the exoskeleton to which are attached spines. Tube feet enable movement, and the spines also help in moving. The mouth is at the base, near the sea floor or rock surface, and it is ringed by a structure like a jaw (which is called Aristotle's lantern), which is used to eat seaweed and to scrape algae from rocks. The shell, or test, can be round, heart-shaped or slightly flattened, and the earlier fossil forms tended to be regular.

Echinoids are very often well preserved (although not with their spines, of course), particularly in the chalk of the Cretaceous. A typical example of a Jurassic echinoid, showing the five-fold organisation is *Clypeus* (figure 24). This is an irregular form and is called a sand dollar. The mouth is at the centre of the test. The five strips resembling petals are the ambulacral areas through which the tube feet protruded. *Hemicidaris* is a very regular echinoid and also possesses rows of tubercles for holding spines. These two examples can be found up to about 10 centimetres in diameter. A common form from the Upper Chalk of the Cretaceous is *Micraster*, a heart-shaped example. The ambulacral areas are sunken and large plates comprise the areas in between.

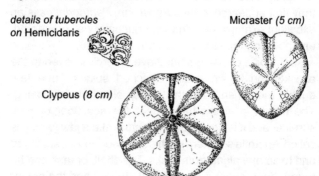

Figure 24: Echinoid fossils

details of tubercles on Hemicidaris

Micraster *(5 cm)*

Clypeus *(8 cm)*

Other groups

There are other invertebrate groups of less significance to the collector, but which are fascinating nevertheless. The *Radiolaria* are minute and similar to the formainifera. They have shells of silica which can be complex and beautiful, and these too form great accumulations of sediment. Other groups include the *Goniatites*, cephalopods similar to the ammonites (but older), and *Bryozoans*, a colonial form with exoskeleton. They are important reef builders, and there are about 5000 species.

Finally, *Ostracods,* although bivalved in appearance, are crustaceans that are used in dating and matching rocks. They first appeared in the Cambrian.

PART SIX

PLANT FOSSILS

It is worthwhile looking briefly at fossil plants as there is a good chance that at some outcrops, particularly from the Carboniferous, you may find leaves, or parts of trunk or roots. Plants can be classified broadly into nonvascular and vascular. Nonvascular plants include mosses and liverworts. These first occurred about 400 million years ago, but they formed low profile plants on the ground because they did not have the structure and support to grow upwards as did the vascular plants.

Vascular plants are divided into those with and without seeds. The seedless plants include the club mosses, horsetails and ferns. The seed plants are further divided into the angiosperms (the flowering plants) and the gymnosperms, which include conifers, cycads and the ginkgo, which, in effect, is a living fossil with only one species living today, even though it was common in the Mesozoic. For the fossil collector, vascular plants are of more interest.

Lycophyta

This division of the seedless vascular plants (lycopods or giant club mosses) contains a particularly good example, *Lepidodendron*, an Upper Carboniferous variety that grew to heights of 30 metres. The trunk at the base could be as much as 2 metres across, and it was a tall tree with branches and leaves at the top. Figure 25 ilustrates a typical fossil form of this plant, which clearly shows the structure. The diamond-like shapes are leaf scars. *Sigillaria* is another trunk from a tree that reached a similar height and ended with a small number of branches with clusters of leaves. *Stigmaria* is part of the root of a lycopod tree. All these fossils are Carboniferous.

Figure 25: Some lycopod plant fossils

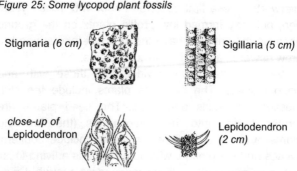

Stigmaria *(6 cm)*

Sigillaria *(5 cm)*

close-up of Lepidodendron

Lepidodendron *(2 cm)*

Sphenophyta

This division includes the horsetails, which have marked joints on their stems. The leaves bush at the top in a circlet formation, and some forms grew up to 12 or 13 metres. It first appeared in the Devonian and is still found today, the larger form in the tropics. *Calamites* (*see* figure 26) is a variety of the Lower Carboniferous to Permian and *Sphenophyllum* illustrates the type of leaves.

Figure 26: Horsetail fossils

Sphenophyllum *(2 cm)*

Calamites
(8 cm)

Gymnosperms

These are the simplest seed plants and in the Carboniferous there were two groups forming trees: the cordaites and the seed ferns. The cordaites grew very tall, and the seed ferns are extinct. The fronds of seed ferns are often found as fossils, e.g. *Neuropteris* (Lower Carboniferous to Permian [*see* figure 27]). *Sphenopteris* is another example (Devonian to Upper Carboniferous).

Figure 27: Seed fern fossils

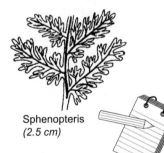

Neuropteris *(each pinnacle or 'leaf' 1 cm)*

Sphenopteris *(2.5 cm)*

PART SEVEN

CONCLUSIONS

This small book has provided a very brief introduction to fossils for the interested amateur. Inevitably, it only scratches the surface and there are many aspects left uncovered, such as vertebrate palaeontology (which admittedly is less likely to be encountered!), and within the group considered only a tiny fraction of the vast numbers of fossil species described have been included. However, for anyone with an interest, or who has had an interest kindled by this book, there are many more sources of information and potentially many, many hours of fascinating hunting and collecting.

Titles in this series: